D1400004

CREATE with
DUCT
TAPE

DUCT TAPE
Fashion

by Carolyn Bernhardt

Lerner Publications • Minneapolis

Lerner Publications Company
A division of Lerner Publishing Group, Inc.
241 First Avenue North
Minneapolis, MN 55401 USA

For reading levels and more information, look up this title at www.lernerbooks.com.

Main body text set in Bembo. Typeface provided by Monotype.

Library of Congress Cataloging-in-Publication Data

Names: Bernhardt, Carolyn, author.
Title: Duct tape fashion / by Carolyn Bernhardt.
Description: Minneapolis : Lerner Publications, [2016] | Series: Create with duct tape | Audience: Ages 7-11. | Audience: Grades 4 to 6. | Includes bibliographical references and index.
Identifiers: LCCN 2016018646 (print) | LCCN 2016020016 (ebook) | ISBN 9781512426694 (lb : alk. paper) | ISBN 9781512427660 (eb pdf)
Subjects: LCSH: Tape craft--Juvenile literature. | Duct tape--Juvenile literature. | Fashion--Juvenile literature. | Handicraft--Juvenile literature.
Classification: LCC TT869.7 .B47 2016 (print) | LCC TT869.7 (ebook) | DDC 745.59--dc23

LC record available at https://lccn.loc.gov/2016018646

Manufactured in the United States of America
1-41458-23340-8/16/2016

Contents

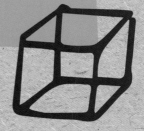

Strong, Sticky, and Stylish

What's strong enough to secure bumpers to cars but soft enough to make a shirt? It's super sticky. It's **waterproof**. It's duct tape!

This amazing material was first known as duck tape. This was because it was great at **repelling** water, similar to a duck's feathers. Soldiers in World War II (1939–1945) used duct tape to repair military vehicles. Later, people used the tape to connect **air ducts**. So, the tape became known as duct tape.

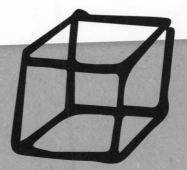

From fixing household items to patching spacecraft, people have found endless uses for duct tape. It has even become a fashion statement. Crafters use it to make tough wallets, waterproof hats, cool **accessories**, and more. This trend has led to an explosion in duct tape crafting possibilities. Today, duct tape comes in a rainbow of colors and patterns. Find your favorite shade and prepare to design your very own duct tape fashions!

Fantastic Fibers

Duct tape's strength comes from its special fibers. These fibers are woven into the tape in a crisscross pattern. They keep duct tape secure under lots of pressure.

Before You
Get Started

Sticky Supply

Duct tape's stickiness makes it great for securing wearables together. No needle and thread are needed to connect pieces. Glue, zippers, and buttons are not necessary either! Crafters can simply stick strips together to create cool clothes and accessories. But this supreme stickiness can also make crafting tricky. As you create cool fashions, work slowly and carefully. This will help you avoid sticking the wrong pieces together.

Workspace and Bases

Before beginning any duct tape fashion project, create a clean workspace. Make sure your tools and materials are in reach. Keep small scraps and supplies organized. Place them on the edges of your work area or in small containers. This will prevent them from sticking to your strips of tape. Before working with base items, such as headbands or clothing, be aware that duct tape may be hard to remove from certain surfaces. It may also leave a sticky **residue** behind once removed. Make sure any items that will be covered in duct tape are okay to use.

Fashion Imagination

Fashion is whatever you make it! The same goes for duct tape fashion. As you craft with this super tape, get creative. What would happen if you added another layer? How would your piece change if you included more colors? Think about how to add your own twists. Find new ways to tear, fold, connect, or convert duct tape into stylish shapes and one-of-a-kind wearables. Use your imagination. Then tear and stick to make duct tape creations you're proud to wear.

Stay Safe

When **designing** and wearing duct tape items, safety is most important. Check with an adult before you try these duct tape activities. Never stick duct tape's sticky side directly to skin. Do not place duct tape on your or someone else's face. Never place it over eyes, ears, or mouths. And never bind any body part with duct tape. Finally, be careful when using sharp objects, such as scissors.

Cool Cuffs

Design sturdy cuffs to decorate your wrists in dashing duct tape!

Materials

- scissors
- cardboard tube
- duct tape

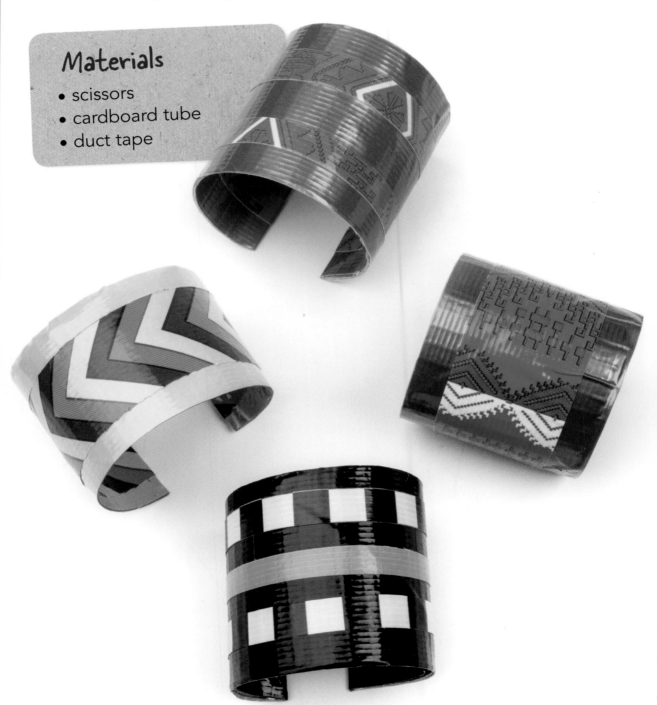

1 Carefully cut a slit along the side of the tube. This will allow the cuffs to be opened over your wrist.

2 Wrap a strip of duct tape around the cardboard tube.

3 Cut along the edge of the strip. Put tape over the edges of the ends. Your cuff is now ready to wear!

4 Repeat Steps 1 through 3, making your way down the tube. Use strips with different patterns to make a variety of fun cuffs!

5 Decorate your cool cuffs in different colors. Wear them together to make a wrist rainbow!

Did You Know?

Nuclear Grade Duct Tape can handle temperatures of up to 200°Fahrenheit (93.3°Celsius).

Woven Ring

Weave a mini duct tape braid to make a vibrant ring!

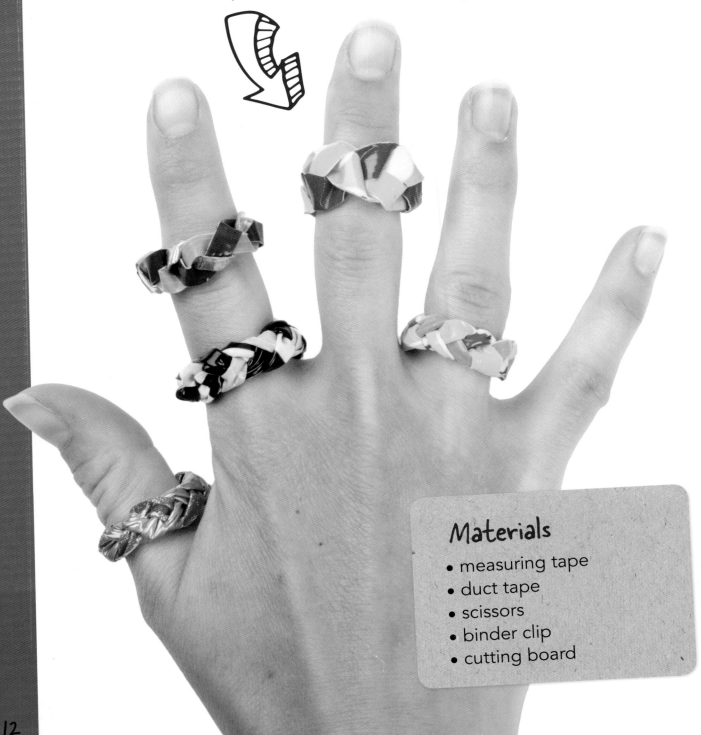

Materials
- measuring tape
- duct tape
- scissors
- binder clip
- cutting board

 1 Measure around your finger with a measuring tape. Add 1 inch (2.5 centimeters) to the measurement. Cut a strip of duct tape twice as long as the total measurement.

 2 Fold the strip in half the short way, pressing the sticky sides together. Then cut it into thin, even strips. Cut strips of other colors the same way.

2

 3 Clip the ends of three strips to the top of the cutting board.

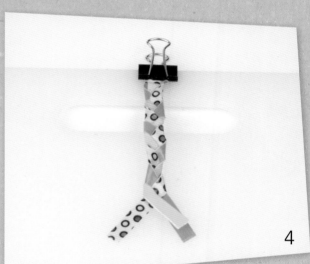

 4 Braid the strips together. Use small strips of tape to secure the ends of the braid.

 5 Wrap the braid around your finger to make sure it fits. Then tape your ring into a loop. Your little tape ring is complete! It slips on and off easily, it's waterproof, and it will never rust!

4

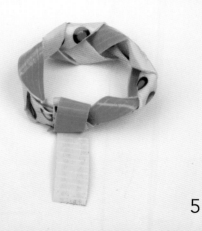

5

Sticky Tip

To braid, you must work in sets of three. Secure all three strips with a binder clip at the top. Pull one outside strip over the middle strip, making it the new middle strip. Repeat this step with the other outside strip. Keep moving your outside strips to the middle, switching between them as you go. Secure your braid with more tape!

Trusty Tape Belt

Build a bright belt that is as functional as it is fashionable!

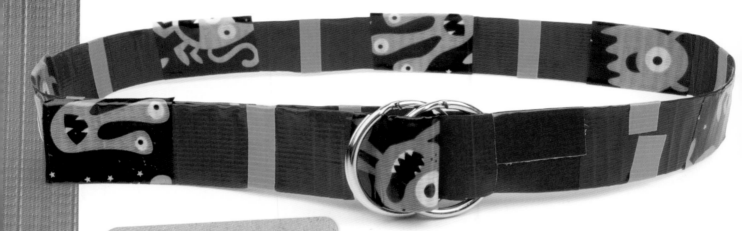

Materials

- measuring tape
- duct tape
- scissors
- 2 key rings

1

 Measure around your waist with a measuring tape. Add 2 inches (5 cm) to the measurement. Cut a strip of duct tape as long as the total measurement.

 Fold the tape in half the long way, pressing the sticky sides together. This creates a skinny belt.

3

 Slip the key rings onto one end of the belt. Fold the end of the belt over the rings. Tape that end in place.

 Decorate your belt! Then thread it through the belt loops on your pants. Pull the end of the belt through both rings.

 Fold the belt over one ring but through the next. Thread the tail end through the belt loops. Pull until comfortable. Wear your new duct tape belt to hold up your pants with style!

4

Did You Know?

Duct tape's strong fabric backing is called scrim.

Stylish
Hair Bow

Tie a bright bow with duct tape
for a bit of hair flair!

Materials
- measuring tape
- duct tape
- scissors
- strong, quick-setting glue
- hair clip, headband, or hair elastic

2

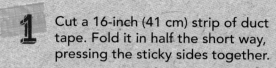
Cut a 16-inch (41 cm) strip of duct tape. Fold it in half the short way, pressing the sticky sides together.

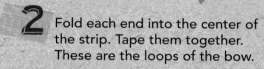
Fold each end into the center of the strip. Tape them together. These are the loops of the bow.

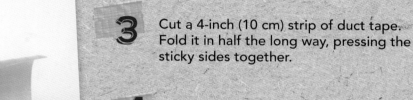

3

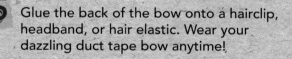
Cut a 4-inch (10 cm) strip of duct tape. Fold it in half the long way, pressing the sticky sides together.

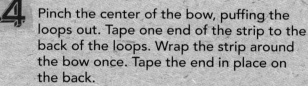
Pinch the center of the bow, puffing the loops out. Tape one end of the strip to the back of the loops. Wrap the strip around the bow once. Tape the end in place on the back.

Glue the back of the bow onto a hairclip, headband, or hair elastic. Wear your dazzling duct tape bow anytime!

4

Fringed
Feather
Charms

Form feathers out of duct tape. Then turn these fringed pieces into charms that will infuse fun into your favorite outfit!

Materials
- duct tape
- measuring tape
- scissors
- marker
- pushpin
- optional: earring hooks, key ring, or necklace chain

1 Cut a 12-inch (30.5 cm) strip of duct tape. Fold the strip in half the short way, pressing the sticky sides together.

2 Draw a feather shape on the strip. Cut out the feather.

3 Cut fringe along each side of the feather to make it look as real as possible!

4 Use the pushpin to poke a hole in the feather's stem. Then thread a key ring, earring hook, or necklace chain through the hole. Secure with a small strip of tape, if needed.

5 Repeat steps 1 through 4 to make more charms. Experiment with different colors and shapes. Your fringed charms are light as a feather but super tough. Wear them anywhere!

Duct Tape
Necktie

Whip up a duct tape necktie that will make any outfit fabulously formal!

Materials
- duct tape
- scissors
- pin back

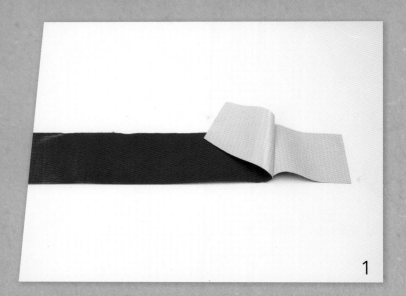

 Cut two strips of tape the length of your **forearm**. Carefully lay one on top of the other, pressing the sticky sides together.

 Tie a knot near one end of the strip. Cut off the short tail. The long tail is the back of the tie.

 Cut two strips of duct tape 2 inches (5 cm) longer than the length of your forearm. Lay one on top of the other, pressing the sticky sides together. This will be the front of the tie. Decorate it however you'd like!

 Trim the ends of the tie front into points. Do the same to the back. Then tuck one end of the tie front into the knot. Secure with a small strip of tape.

 Tape a pin back to the back of the tie's knot. Pin your cool tape tie to any shirt or sweater for instant style!

Shoe Redo

Perform fashion magic on an old pair of shoes with stylish duct tape strips and shapes!

Materials
- pair of old shoes
- duct tape
- scissors
- measuring tape
- optional: hot glue and hot glue gun

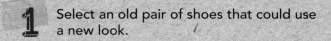

1 Select an old pair of shoes that could use a new look.

2 Remove the laces from the shoes. Then cover each shoe with strips of tape. Make sure not to cover the **eyelets**. Cut slits into the tape to help it fold over curves without creasing.

1

3 Cut six strips of duct tape 12 inches (30.5 cm) long. Roll them up the long way. Make the rolls thin enough so they are thin enough to fit through the eyelets of the shoes. Start threading a strip through the eyelets. Tape strips to the ends as necessary to make the laces long enough.

2

4 Add fun details to your shoes. With an adult's help, hot glue duct tape braids along the edges. Add a duct tape feather to the side, or attach duct tape bows to the toes. Then step out into the world and show off your shoe redo!

3

Did You Know?

The largest duct tape fashion show in the world was held in Avon, Ohio, in 2014. More than 300 people participated.

Tape
Tote Bag

Take your things anywhere in your trendy tape tote!

Materials
- duct tape
- scissors
- measuring tape

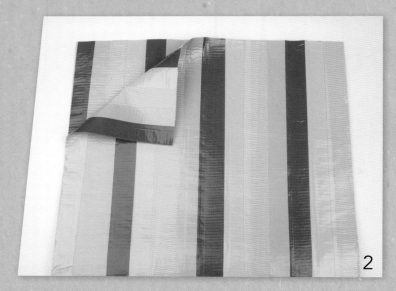

 Cut twenty-eight strips of duct tape 30 inches (76 cm) long. Overlap the long edge of one strip slightly with the long edge of another strip. Keep them sticky-side up. Repeat with the remaining strips until you've formed a rectangle.

 Fold the rectangle in half the long way, pressing the sticky sides together. Then fold the sheet in half the short way.

 Cut a strip of tape 36 inches (91 cm) long. Fold it in half the short way, pressing the sticky sides together. Then cut the strip in half the long way. These are your handles!

 Tape the handles to the inside of the bag on either side.

 Secure the sides of your bag with tape. Fill your bag with books, sports equipment, groceries, craft supplies, and more!

Total Tape
T-shirt

Tear, connect, fold, and form an
entire shirt from duct tape!

Materials
- T-shirt
- duct tape
- scissors
- permanent marker

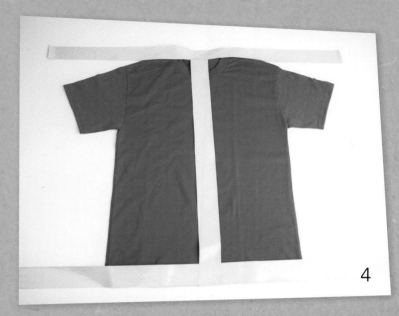

4

5

6

1 Select a T-shirt that's a little bit big for you. Lay it flat.

2 Cut two strips of duct tape long enough to go from the collar of your shirt to the hem.

3 Cut two strips of tape long enough to go from the edge of one sleeve all the way to the other.

4 Arrange the strips into an uppercase *I* shape, sticky sides up. Attach the vertical strip to the horizontal strips.

5 Remove the shirt. Fill in the *I* shape with strips of tape, creating a rectangle. Overlap the edge of each strip slightly. Keep the sticky sides facing up.

6 Create a second rectangle the exact same size. Carefully lay one rectangle on top of the other, pressing the sticky sides together.

Total Tape T-shirt continued next page

7 Repeat steps 2 through 6 to make a matching sheet of tape. This will be the other side of the shirt.

 8 Lay the T-shirt on one of the tape sheets. Trace around it. Cut it out. Repeat this step with the other sheet.

 9 Lay one T-shirt shape on top of the other. Tape along the seams. Leave holes for the sleeves, the collar, and the bottom of the shirt.

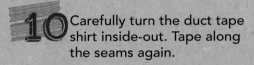 **10** Carefully turn the duct tape shirt inside-out. Tape along the seams again.

 11 Decorate your shirt however you want. Mix it up with fun patterns, shapes, and colors. Try making some matching duct tape pants. Then flaunt your terrific tape T-shirt wherever you go!

9

10

Dress to Impress with Duct Tape!

Your fashion-forward clothes are ready to shine! Take them for a spin in a fashion show with your friends and family. Or, test out your tote at the library. How many books can it hold? Are other readers jealous of your innovation? Make more bags of all shapes and sizes for your many different adventures. Wherever you go, dress yourself in your duct tape creations to make a sparkling statement to everyone around you!

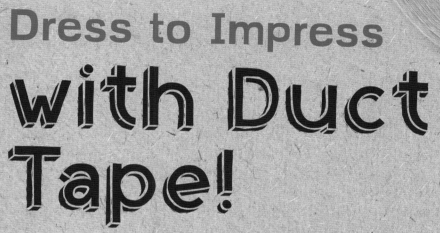

Cleanup and Safekeeping

Now that you've created these cool fashions, it's time to clean up. Store duct tape rolls out of the sun. Throw away any ruined strips, or save them for a future fashion addition.

To care for your newly created pieces, store them out of the sun or direct heat. If the tape gets too hot, its glue can become gummy. If any of your items become broken from wear, patch and repair them with more tape.

Keep Creating!

Duct tape can turn ordinary clothes extraordinary. The projects you created are just the beginning. What other wearables could you make from this terrific tape? Dream up your own wild looks and keep creating!

Glossary

accessories: small items that you wear with your clothes

air ducts: pipes that move air around buildings

design: to draw a plan for something that can be made

eyelets: small holes in a shoe for a shoelace to pass through

forearm: the part of the arm between the elbow and the wrist

fringed: bordered with cords or threads

repelling: driving off or keeping something away

residue: what remains after something else is removed or completed

waterproof: designed to prevent water from entering

Further Information

Berne, Emma Carlson. *Jewelry Tips & Tricks*
Minneapolis: Lerner Publications, 2016.
Use basic tools to create simple, stylish jewelry for every occasion.

DK findout!: Fashion
http://www.dkfindout.com/us/history/fashion
Learn about the history of US fashion with this interesting, interactive timeline.

Duct Tape Crafts: Fashion
http://duckbrand.com/craft -decor#row=6&type=Fashion
Try out trendy crafts tested by one of the most famous duct tape companies.

Morgan, Richela Fabian. *Tape It & Wear It: 60 Duct-Tape Activities to Make and Wear.*
Hauppauge, NY: Barron's Educational Series, 2014.
Add to your duct tape wardrobe with these additional fashion crafts.

Index

Photo Acknowledgments

The images in this book are used with the permission of: © Aleksander Kaczmarek/iStockphoto, p. 29 (girl); © Feng Yu/Shutterstock Images, pp. 1 (gray tape roll), 5 (gray tape roll), 8 (gray tape roll), 13 (gray tape roll), 29 (gray tape roll); © Jupiterimages/Stockbyte/Thinkstock, p. 9; © Katy McDonnell/DigitalVision/Thinkstock, p. 7 (girl); © mama_mia/Shutterstock Images, pp. 3, 10, 11, 12, 14, 16, 17, 18, 20, 22, 23, 24, 26, 29, 30; © Mckenna_Ringwald/iStockphoto, p. 8; © Mighty Media, Inc., pp. 1 (gray tape), 1 (green tape), 2, 4 (zebra tape), 5 (green tape), 5 (blue tape), 5 (shoe craft), 6 (bag craft), 6 (purple tape), 7 (blue tape), 7 (leopard print tape), 8 (cuffs craft), 8 (blue tape), 8 (purple tape), 8 (tie-dye tape), 9 (red tape), 10 (blue tape), 10 (cuffs craft), 11 (top), 11 (middle), 11 (bottom), 11 (blue tape), 11 (green tape), 12 (rings craft), 12 (purple tape), 13 (top), 13 (middle), 13 (bottom), 13 (purple tape), 14 (tape rolls), 14 (belt craft), 14 (red tape), 15 (top), 15 (middle), 15 (bottom), 15 (red tape), 15 (green tape), 16 (bow craft), 16 (blue tape), 16 (purple tape), 17 (top), 17 (middle), 17 (bottom), 17 (blue tape), 18 (feather crafts), 18 (purple tape), 19 (top), 19 (middle), 19 (bottom), 19 (purple tape), 20 (tie craft), 20 (red tape), 21 (top), 21 (middle), 21 (bottom), 21 (red tape), 22 (shoe craft), 22 (blue tape), 23 (top), 23 (middle), 23 (bottom), 23 (blue tape), 23 (green tape), 24 (bag craft), 24 (purple tape), 25 (top), 25 (middle), 25 (bottom), 25 (purple tape), 26 (shirt craft), 26 (red tape), 27 (top), 27 (middle), 27 (bottom), 27 (red tape), 28 (top), 28 (bottom), 28 (red tape), 29 (blue tape), 29 (purple tape), 29 (red tape), 29 (zebra tape), 30 (tie-dye tape), 31 (purple tape), 32 (leopard tape), 32 (red tape); © wongwean/Shutterstock Images, pp. 4 (blue paper), 6 (green paper), 13 (green paper), 15 (blue paper), 19 (green paper), 21 (blue paper), 25 (green paper), 27 (blue paper), 28 (blue paper), 30 (green paper).

Cover: © Feng Yu/Shutterstock Images (gray tape roll); © Mighty Media, Inc.; © wongwean/Shutterstock Images (blue background).

Back Cover: © Feng Yu/Shutterstock Images (gray tape roll); © wongwean/Shutterstock Images (blue background).